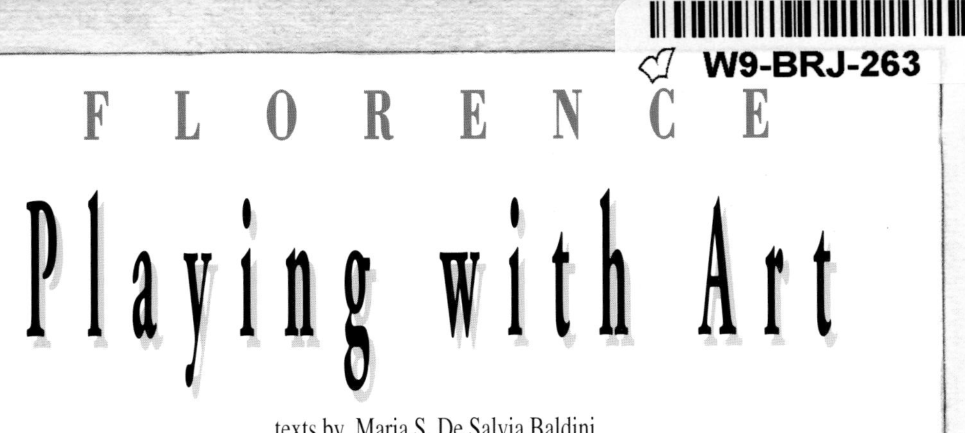

FLORENCE
Playing with Art

texts by Maria S. De Salvia Baldini
illustrations by Paola Boldrini

Mandragora

50122 Firenze - Piazza Duomo, 9

Graphic design: Lorenzo Gualtieri
Translation: Erika Pauli, Studio Comunicare
Photographs: La Mandragora Archives,
Liberto Perugi, Antonio Quattrone
Photolithography: Studio Leonardo-Firenze
Printing: Alpi Lito - Firenze

For small children their first encounter with the world of art is a colorful magical experience whether they are face to face with the masterworks themselves, or whether they meet them in the pages of an art book - a book like this one perhaps which takes the work of art off its pedestal and brings it into the daily life and play of even the smallest of children, giving their imagination free rein. The works of art are no longer distant objects, hard to understand and maybe even boring, but multicolored tools which can help them understand the story of our civilization.

In pages made to measure for the small hands of the readers, great art scales down to their size and opens up its enchanted universe for those who want to enter. That mysterious place called museum turns into a new still undiscovered world - full of hidden treasures - a treasure trove of art.

Florence is a city full of works of art.
Many of them are to be found in the museums, places so strange and magic they make us want to discover them and begin a new delightful game -
a fascinating adventure with a thousand colors: the yellow of the sun, the blue of the sea, the green of meadows, the red of sunset - all the colors of life and of art.

Venus, the goddess of love and beauty,
was born from the crystal
clear waters of the ocean,
and the painter shows her
as she
is gently blown to shore by the winds.

The Birth of Venus

She is a beautiful princess dressed only in her long blonde hair: a handmaiden brings her a cloak, covered with marvelous flowers, to clothe her.

With his small hands, an angel strums the strings of a mandolin that is almost as big as he is.
Two great colored wings frame his saucy little face.

Musician Ange

It almost seems as if the echo of his music sets him day-dreaming: maybe he is thinking of his peaceful world and his joyous flights among golden clouds.

The Battle of San Romano

The painter is telling us about a real war that was fought between Siena and Florence and that was won by the Florentines. But the fantastically colored knights and horses in his painted battle seem to be living in an enchanted world.

The horses on the ground don't at all look as if they were wounded but as if they were asleep; lances, trumpets, halberds and plumes, also in brilliant colors, take us back into the world of fables.

The elegant Duchess Battista Sforza is wearing precious jewels. Pearls and veils are worked into her elaborate hair-do in line with the fashions of the time. Behind her is a lovely landscape.

Her husband Federico wears a typical hat of the times and a fine bright red jacket. Even so, what one notes most is his hooked nose, the result of a sword blow in battle.

Bacchus

Bacchus is the god of wine: that's why he wears a wreath of grapes and grape leaves in his hair. The boy we are looking at is really one of the painter's assistants who decided to have fun and draped a white sheet over his shoulder as disguise.
Then he sat down in front of a basket of fruit and picked up a glass of wine to offer to a guest.

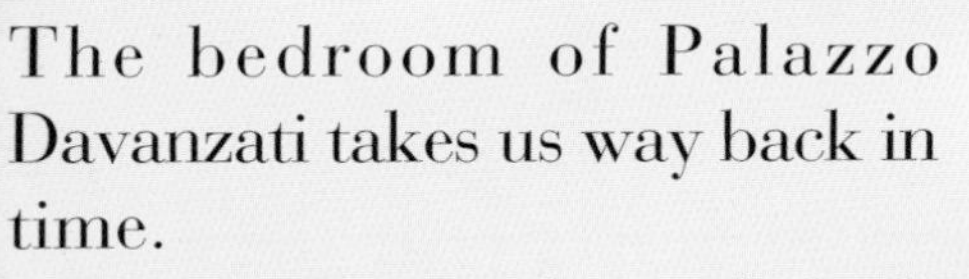

The bedroom of Palazzo Davanzati takes us way back in time.
Let's tiptoe in and quietly look around: if we try hard enough we can almost hear the voices of the children who lived here so many years ago, crying in their cradle or making a racket as they jump around on the big double bed. They must have had lots of fun playing hide and seek in these enormous houses: the staircases and the kitchens were huge and on various floors.
Often though, because it was cold and there was no central heating, they played quietly next to the fireplace with their dolls and rocking horses.

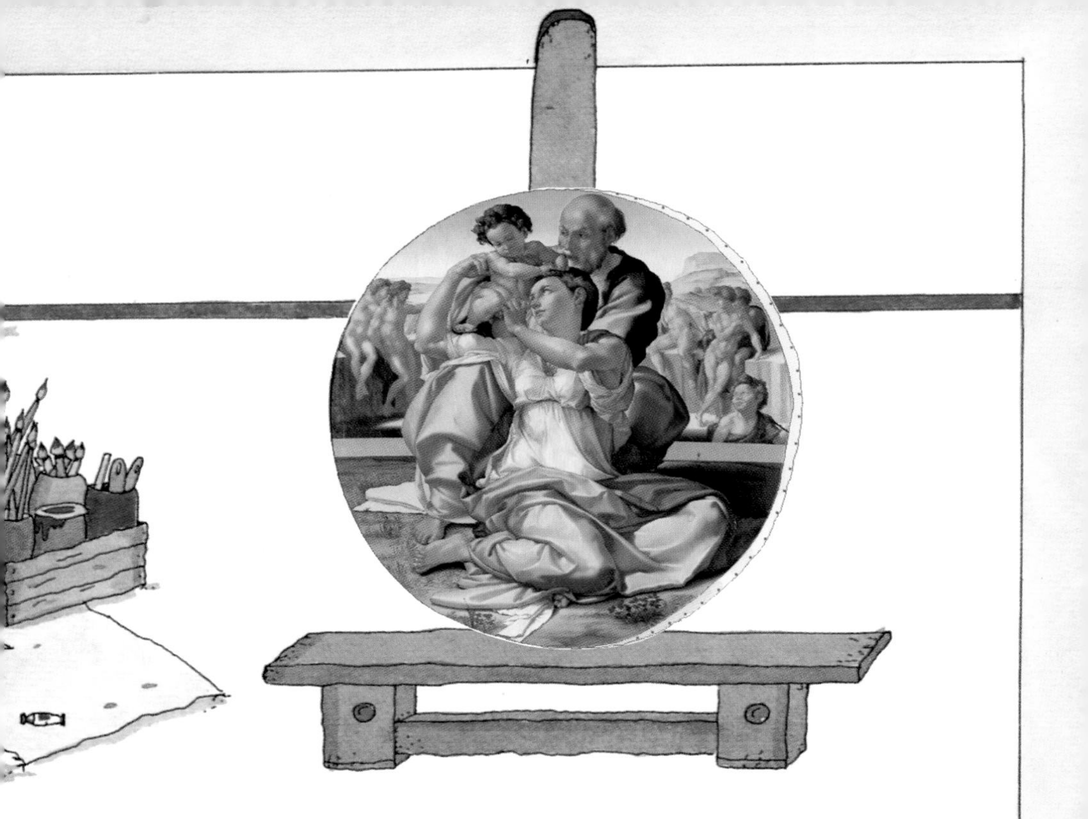

Mary, Joseph and Jesus are resting on the Flight to Egypt. They had to leave home when Herod, king of Judea, ordered his soldiers to kill all small children. Now that the danger is past, the baby wants to be cuddled by his mother.

The size of this nude curly-haired boy is what impresses us first of all, for this white marble statue is more than four meters high.
His name is David and he almost seems to be looking around for a mirror in which to admire himself.

Actually he is full of strength and courage: a true hero who, armed with nothing but his sling-shot, kills the bad giant Goliath.

This is why David is now a symbol of Florence and a gigantic example of beauty.

A splendid Eleonora and her charming son Giovanni gaze out at us as they pose for the painter: her hands are long and white, his are small and chubby.

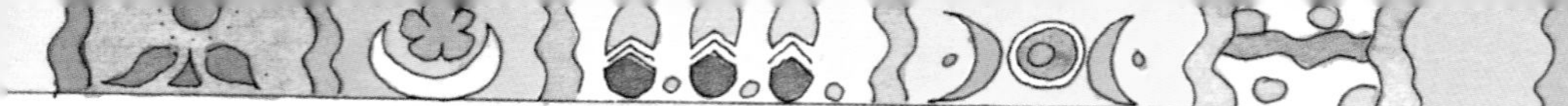

The child's bright eyes and his fine collar slightly askew show us that what he really wants to do is move and play rather than sitting still for the painter.

The little girl with her mischievous air is ready to play shuttlecock, which is what tennis was called in those days. To be sure her racket and ball are not quite like those of today, but she certainly must have had just as much fun. What a shame though that children, like the girl in the picture, had to wear complicated clothes like those of their parents.

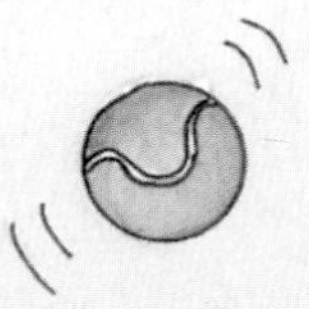

Little girls in particular had the most uncomfortable clothes, with tight blouses and full skirts, often completed by charming bonnets which were not very practical.

Children dance and sing in a merry ring-around-the-rosies; they happily hold hands and sing at the tops of their voices, although some seem to be a bit more timid than others.

They look like angels without wings, light even if they are in marble.

This famous crucifix, even though it is anything but small, should be observed through a magnifying glass.

What is left after the Arno flooded and washed away a great deal of the painted surface, is really not very much. But it has been patiently restored and today we can still get an idea of how beautiful it once was.

The Chimera, a fantastic monster with the head of a lion, the body of a goat, and a serpent for a tail, looks like an enormous cat; with its jaws wide open, it is ready to defend itself by attacking.

The animal has been wounded and its expression shows what pain it is in.

There's a marvelous secret to be discovered about this young man, shown as he is sculpting a work of art.

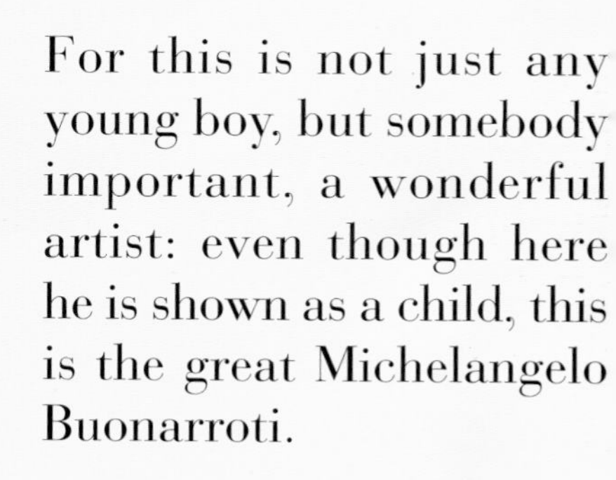

For this is not just any young boy, but somebody important, a wonderful artist: even though here he is shown as a child, this is the great Michelangelo Buonarroti.

A

Pleasant encounters can be made both with nature and with art in the Boboli Gardens: soft grass, fragrant flowers, elegant statues, gushing fountains and mysterious grottos.

Lorenzo dei Medici, known as the Magnificent, is shown here as a boy riding a fine white horse.
Even as a boy, so goes the story, he was intelligent and ambitious, as well as generous and sensitive: he was already writing poetry at twelve.

List of

Room of Venus
Palazzo Pitti
(1438-1850 ca.)

Sandro Botticelli (1445-1510),
The Birth of Venus (1485 ca.).
Galleria degli Uffizi

Rosso Fiorentino (1495-1540),
Musician Angel (1522 ca.).
Galleria degli Uffizi

Paolo Uccello (1397-1475),
The Battle of San Romano
(1456 ca.). Galleria degli Uffizi

Vorks

Piero della Francesca (1416-1492),
Portraits of Battista Sforza and of Federico da Montefeltro or Diptych of the Dukes of Urbino
(1465-70 ca.). Galleria degli Uffizi

Caravaggio (1573-1610), **Bacchus.**
(1589 ca.)
Galleria degli Uffizi

Michelangelo Buonarroti
(1475-1564),
Holy Family or **Doni Tondo**
(1506-1508).
Galleria degli Uffizi

Bedroom in walnut,
Nineteenth-century reconstruction.
Palazzo Davanzati, Museo dell'antica casa fiorentina

Bronzino (1503-1572).
Portrait of Eleonora of Toledo and her Son Giovanni (1545-46).
Galleria degli Uffizi

Jean Baptiste-Siméon Chardin (1699-1779).
Girl with a Shuttlecock
Galleria degli Uffizi

Michelangelo Buonarroti (1475-1564),
David (1502-04).
Galleria dell'Accademia

Luca della Robbia (1400-1482),
Choir loft panel (1433-39).
Museo dell'Opera del Duomo

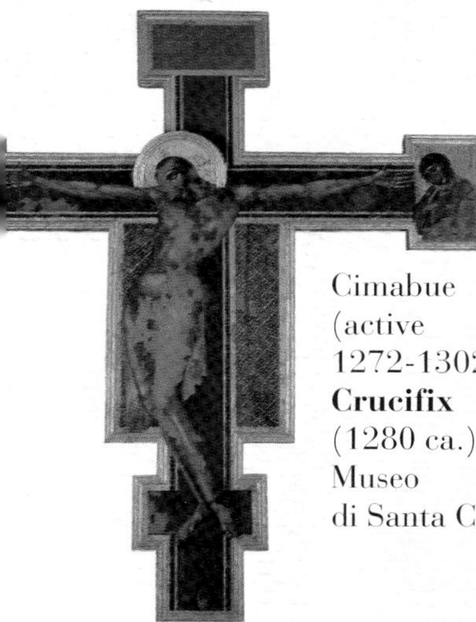

Cimabue
(active
1272-1302),
Crucifix
(1280 ca.).
Museo
di Santa Croce

The Chimera of Arezzo,
Etruscan bronze
(second half 5th cent. B.C.-
first half 4th cent. B.C.).
Museo Archeologico

Cesare Zocchi
(1777-1850),
**Michelangelo
as a boy.**
Casa Buonarroti

Neptune's Pool
Boboli Gardens
(1550-1790 ca.)

Benozzo Gozzoli (1420-
1497)
**The Procession of the
Three Kings**
(1459-60) detail
Palazzo Medici-Riccardi,
Cappella dei Magi